The Second Buddha Walk

D1596347

Nirala Series
The Second Buddha Walk

Recipient of fellowships and grants from The Rockefeller Foundation, Ireland Literature Exchange, Trubar Foundation, Slovenia, The Institute for the Translation of Hebrew Literature and The Foundation for the Production and Translation of Dutch Literature, Yuyutsu RD Sharma is an internationally acclaimed South Asian poet and translator.

He has published nine poetry collections including, *A Blizzard in my Bones: New York Poems* (Nirala, 2016), *Quaking Cantos: Nepal Earthquake Poems,* (Nirala, 2016), *Milarepa's Bones, 33 New Poems,* (Nirala, 2012), *Nepal Trilogy, Photographs and Poetry on Annapurna, Everest, Helambu & Langtang* (www.Nepal-Trilogy.de, Epsilonmedia, Karlsruhe, 2010), a 900-page book with renowned German photographer, Andreas Stimm, *Space Cake, Amsterdam, & Other Poems from Europe and America,* (2009, Indian reprint 2014) and *Annapurna Poems,* 2008, Reprint, 2012, 2018).

Yuyutsu also brought out a translation of Irish poet Cathal O' Searcaigh poetry in Nepali in a bilingual collection entitled, *Kathmandu: Poems, Selected and New* (2006) and a translation of Hebrew poet Ronny Someck's poetry in Nepali in a bilingual edition, *Baghdad, February 1991 & Other Poems.* He has translated and edited several anthologies of contemporary Nepali poetry in English, most recently the Himalayan Arts Folio of American magazine, *Drunken Boat,* and launched a literary movement, *Kathya Kayakalpa* (Content Metamorphosis) in Nepali poetry.

Three books of his poetry, *Poemes de l' Himalayas* (L'Harmattan, Paris), *Poemas de Los Himalayas* (Cosmopoeticia, Cordoba, Spain) and *Jezero Fewa & Konj* (Sodobnost International) have appeared in French, Spanish and Slovenian respectively. In addition, *Eternal Snow: A Worldwide Anthology of One Hundred Twenty-Five Poetic Intersections with Himalayan Poet Yuyutsu RD Sharma* has just appeared.

Widely traveled author, he has read his works at several prestigious places including Poetry Café, London, Seamus Heaney Center for Poetry, Belfast, New York University, New York, The Kring, Amsterdam, P.E.N, Paris, Knox College, Illinois, Whittier College, California, Baruch College, New York, WB Yeats' Center, Sligo, Shi Shangzhuang, Hebei, China, Gustav Stressemann Institute, Bonn, Rubin Museum, New York, Cosmopoetica, Cordoba, Spain, Beijing International Book Fair, The Irish Writers' Centre, Dublin, Columbia University, New York, Lu Xun Literary Institute, Beijing, The Guardian Newsroom, London, Trois Rivieres Poetry Festival, Quebec, Arnofini, Bristol, Borders, London, FIP, Buenos Aires, Slovenian Book Days, Ljubljana, Royal Society of Dramatic Arts, London, Gunter Grass House, Bremen, GTZ, Kathmandu, International Poetry Festival, Granada, Nicaragua, Nehru Center, London, Beijing Normal University, The Beijing Bookworm, Universidad Abierta Interamericana (UAI) / Indian Embassy, Buenos Aires, March Hare, Newfoundland, Canada, Gannon University, Erie, Frankfurt Book Fair, Frankfurt, Sahitya Academy, New Delhi, Indian International Center, New Delhi, and Villa Serbelloni, Italy.

He has held workshops in creative writing and translation at Queen's University, Belfast, University of Ottawa and South Asian Institute, Heidelberg University, Germany, University of California, Davis, Sacramento State University, California, Beijing Open University and New York University, New York.

His works have appeared in *Poetry Review, Chanrdrabhaga, Sodobnost, Amsterdam Weekly, Indian Literature, Irish Pages, Delo, Modern Poetry in Translation, Exiled Ink, Iton77, Little Magazine, The Telegraph, Indian Express* and *Asiaweek.*

The Library of Congress has nominated his book of Nepali translations entitled *Roaring Recitals; Five Nepali Poets* as Best Book of the Year 2001 from Asia under the Program, A World of Books International Perspectives.

"The 'blinding snows of the Annapurnas ridge' inspire a poetry that confronts natural magnificence with exuberant humanity. Yuyutsu R D Sharma's generous vision embraces not only the landscape and its people but the lesser fauna, like the pigeons that speak 'a kind of hushed speech that robbers might use' and the mules on the Tibetan salt route, exhausted and bow-legged from hauling 'cartons of Iceberg, mineral water bottles,/ solar heaters, Chinese tiles, tin cans...' These vividly colored, muscular and energetic poems have an atmosphere of freshness, as though the snow itself had rinsed and brightened them. Like the 'waterfall beds that/ smelled of the birth of fresh fish', they have the tangy, dust-free odor of language born of lived experience."
—**Carol Rumens**, *United Kingdom*

"Formed by 20th century South Asian and North American poetry movements and himself a verbal renewer of his country's literature, he indefatigably writes along rivers and paths, mountains, valleys and villages, verse after verse, one image after the other, an encounter at a time.
—**Dr. Christoph Emmrich,** *Professor of South and Southeast Asian Buddhism, University of Toronto.*

"Yuyutsu RD Sharma brings the bracing airs of the Himalayas to any city. His vigorous, expansive and elemental poems leave Yeti tracks on the streets and mule trails on the Tube. They are packed with rapturous couplings of the urban and the feral."
—**Pascale Petit**, *United Kingdom*

"To do justice to the landscapes and peoples of the highest mountains in the world requires a sensitivity and skill not given to all of us. Andreas Stimm and Yuyutsu R. D. Sharma have succeeded, in this trilogy of photographs and poems, in bringing to life an extraordinary region in all its striking beauty and natural harmony. The unique combination of their photographic and poetic skills succeeds in laying bare the very soul of the Himalayas, the smiling warmth of its inhabitants and its dramatically beautiful peaks and valleys. Each page transports you to a magical and timeless world which, alas, is condemned slowly to disappear as modernization, new roads, and environmental degradation combine to depopulate these remote areas."

—**His Excellency Mr. Keith George Bloomfield,** *Former British Ambassador to Nepal*

Each poem is a delight in itself, a discovery, a new turn of phrase, a new sensation, a world of sound and light, and visions all colliding against each other to provide an unexpected and haunting experience.

—**David Clark** in *Exiled Ink, London*

Yuyutsu RD lives close to Everest. His poetry climbs mountains, swims in rivers and paints the falling leaves in copper. This tango with nature also occurs when Yuyutsu RD closes the window for a moment...

—**Ronny Someck** in *Iton77, Tel Aviv*

A fiercely sublime poet ...the book confirms an enormous talent, as well as purity of purpose with which he approaches his calling. Lines jump out, burning themselves into your consciousness.

—**Amsterdam Weekly**

With this buoyantly audacious work, Yuyutsu RD should be assured of his place in the canon of Asian poetry.

In this new volume he conveys the people and places, the flora and fauna of the Annapurna area of Nepal with an exhilaratingly fresh vision. It is poetry where pastoral elegy becomes fused with magic realism; where earthy common-sense mysticism becomes interlaced with a lush sexuality. The book is a voluptuous and loving evocation of Nepal and I admire its dramatic intensity.

—**Cathal O Searcaigh, Ireland**

The Second Buddha Walk

Inspired by
The Second Buddha: Master of Time Exhibit
at Rubin Museum, New York

Yuyutsu Sharma

Nirala

Nirala Publications
4637/20, Unit no 310, Third Floor,
Hari Sadan,, Ansari Road
Daryaganj, New Delhi-110002
niralabooks@yahoo.co.in
www.niralapublications.com

ISBN-81-8250-098-2

First Edition 2019

Copyright ©Yuyutsu Sharma

Cover Design : Tarun Saxena

Cover Image: Padmasambhava
Tibet; 19th century
Ground Mineral Pigment on Cotton
Rubin Museum of Art
Gift of Shelley and Donald Rubin
C2006.66.530 (HAR 1003))

Printed at
Jaico Offset Printers
New Delhi-110002

For my late father.
Madan Lal Sharma

INTRODUCTION

Icons of Time and Space

New York triggers action, there's no space for gloom in the first city of the world. I lie in my apartment by the Hudson River, nostalgic, the taste of the Himalayan rivers I have left behind ripe in my mouth. It's a Friday and there is NYC Museum Mile Walk and a Free Friday at The Rubin Museum. I go to the newly-opened Giacometti show and reeling under the spell of Swiss master's sleek sculptures take a subway train to go to The Rubin Museum. An Exhibit there on Padamsambhava, also known as Second Buddha hurls me into action. Right there I start working on a long poem on the life and times of the Buddhist saint who in 8th century visited Tibet via Nepal and converted 'Red-faced' Tibetans into Buddhists.

On entering the museum I hear notes of old Bollywood songs blaring, distracting me from the somber mood I came in to overcome homesickness. But as I go up, it is quieter and somehow healing. I see a Tagore related Otolith Movement show at Fourth Floor conjoined to supplement The Second Buddha Show on the top floor. I have read as Guest Speaker here several times and will read my work-in-progress on the 5th of December this year.

On the floor I see Padamsambhava images in gold and earth colors all over. In one of the images, an almost nude disciple/consort is seen sitting the lap of a blue-bodied Bharab-like Padma. His legend of possessing magical powers to subdue the local deities and making them protectors by oath to protect Buddhist faith in Tibet can be seen in the several mandalas hanging on the opposite wall. Padam is said to have made the Tibetan princess his disciple, enraging the king who orders the guru and his daughter to be tied to the stake and burnt alive. Miraculously both survive and nine days after, the oil of the pyre turns into water and the couple appears on a lotus floating in a lake. The miraculous event brings a change in the king's heart who later converts to Buddhism. Thus, Padmasambahava becomes renowned as the Lake-born Vajra, Tsokye Dorje with vajra referring to his indestructible powers.

In another image to my left I see Padma portrayed as Pema Jungne. The painting is layered with stories and exploits of the Guru's life and major events, his early phase as a student in Bodhgaya and a teacher in Tri Songdetsen in Tibet. In addition, he is seen as Lang Palgyi Yeshi performing a ritual to subdue negative spirits fleeing from a triangular ghost trap. The figure is seen wielding a dagger, holding a bell, while his attendant carries a sword, offering cakes (Torma), a bow and arrow and a magical horn.

The marvelous iconography of these images repeatedly brings forth the essential motif of time and space as seen in the Buddhist iconography in the Exhibit. I follow an American tour guide leading a western group and affectionately listen to his loud musings on the events in Padma's life that took place in Nepal, Bhutan and India. I introduce myself to the guide, and learn he has spent time in Nepal as a student. The icons reflect, he announces, a curious fusion of past, present and future. Ancient Tibetans believed that future is what we make it today and it's interwoven with the past while concurrently being anchored in the present. At the end of ninth century as the Tibetan empire fragmented, they looked at the glorious past as a frame of reference for the present and the future. They felt past and present entwined within individual lives. Padma's life, anecdotes and iconography reveals this framework of time and space.

In yet another image, Padma is shown holding a basket, the treasure trove, also in the local language called terton that the Himalayas master left with his disciples, foreseeing a trouble with his faith in future. Padma is said to have shared with his disciples several treasure troves in forms of mantra, object, a vision or a revelation that they centuries after could dig out or conjure if needed. The connection between Padmaambhava and treasure revealers in this or previous lives forges a link between past and the present.

Thus the Second Buddha motif emerges referring to Padmasambhava as the Second Buddha and represents the way in which past can become present. In another painting, the recognition of one of Padma's disciples, named Tangtong Gyelpo, is drawn as an iron chain in his right hand. By building across the Might Rivers, the disciple is said to have transformed the physical landscape of Tibet. Very much the Vedic hymns that the ancient masters wrote and left in the caves for posterity, Padma's shining icons of time and space are treasures to be explored on a daily basis to heal the wounds wrought by nine-eyed demons in our routine lives.

-- **Yuyutsu Sharma**

Contents

"Do not meditate at all, since there is nothing upon which to meditate. Instead, revelation will come through undistracted mindfulness — Since there is nothing by which you can be distracted."

— **Padmasambhava**

The Second Buddha Walk

There's a treasure

There's a treasure
in my warm bed

a velvet touch
of swallows, a scent
of rhododendrons,
two moons and a Sun,
a song of mellowing kisses
I've fantasized
in half a century
of my short life

wild canyons
an abode of snow
a sanctuary
of a million shrines
and jubilant gompas

and down below
a delta of rainforests
where icy waters
of life and longevity flow.

I walk
like an old man...

One

I walk like an old man
I once knew,

grim,
sunken-cheeked,

a face
elegant, stern,

measured,
cautious of each step

wearing nothing
but a Gandhian chuckle

the sharp edge
of a shimmering blade,

a memoir
of racing winds

battering
long bearded trees

in the forest
of rain and rites,

a Lama
of alpine hours

of a drugged itinerary,
ashen visions

of an exhausted mule,
charred moments

of a captured
demigod locked

 in a tantric trance
in the crimson chambers

of Queen's
 inner flesh...

A patch
of earth, soggy

and sanguine
waiting for the kick

of an impending
quake, a terma trove

smashed on
the flagstone steps

of the salt routes
laced with booby traps

woven by
masked demons

of red faced
barbarians...

Two

I walk like an old man
I once knew, I turn around

to enter
my son's study

to find him
dozing on his table.

I sit and watch.
I wait for hours

like someone who
once sat by my side

waiting endlessly
for me to wake up

open my eyes
to listen to the winds

rattling
the doors of his sleep...

Three

I walk like an old man
I once knew, cautious

of each step I take,
counting time on the rainbow

of his rosary,
eyeing the world

meticulously, his body
a fragment of a dingy earth,

ready to accept
the ultimate kick

to roll over
into the depth of an abyss...

Four

I walk like an old man
I once knew, the stupa of his sleep,

a fractured bone
singing by the roaring Himalayan rivers

brooding over the ancient ruins
of a monastery wherein

a pregnant queen lies
dozing by her heirloom of shining galaxies

yak tailed fans stirring
flanks of her luscious nostrils

hallucinating over
the frenzy of rock goddesses hungering for human blood

mountains transforming into
uneven alternates—hedgehog, wild boar,

porcupine, lion, deer.
I see a tingling in the shrine

of my withering skin,
filling the bubble of my body

with a space sound
that shall soon crack open

the pitcher of her dreams
wherein white elephants swirl

fiery shiny alphabets
of newer languages out from

her long lustrous ears...

Five

I walk like an old man
I once knew, asleep on a soft Yeti bed

thinking one day
this frame that I hold

and carry around the globe
like a cracked boat adrift on the hostile waters

will soon turn into
a baby-faced crone

curled up
in a fetal position

under the quiet
quilt of a demigod

in the museum of time,
an effigy of pain and suffering

open to a shameful
public view, a mandala of misfortunes

of a million griefs
and incantations that will soon

retract, unopen
and unwound, and slowly swirl

into my mother's
smoldering eyes as they sloshed

and blood drops
streaked out the moment I lifted

my foot to step over
her moldy threshold

to wander over
the flaming plateaus

like a man before me,
an old man with long dangling earlobes

a frenzy of sullen winds
rocking his headpiece did

the old man
I once knew…

Aama Yangri Hill,
Tarkeghang

A vagabond wind comes
and settles on a hilltop.
It stays there for years, decades,
facing centuries of uproar,
the demon's five fierce thunderclaps.

A wandering wind comes
like Aama Yangri did centuries ago
and begins to build a cairn of beliefs
lifting alphabets like tiny stones
to read Braille of snow and sunlight,
counting time it takes for hot bread
to cool as it comes down
from Tibet with Guru Rinpoche ...

A wandering wind comes
from Tibet like Meme Surya Singhe
to settle on the hilltop.
It finds its face,
its feet and fingers, and its tongue.
But before it can find
the ticking fish of its heart-mind
a dragon with a tongue
long as the tarred road
snaking up the green valleys
appears and kills it.

Mandala

A circular splinter
of light before a wooden hut

a round
clay work of desire

plastered
from the mind's mud

hues
of last night's dreams

the centre pod
sprinkled saffron and vermilion

but the petal
of rhododendron placed

in its centre
shakes as dim-eyed

lorries from
Melamchi Hydro Project

pass by,
spreading a lethal film

of dust
over mandala's miraculous eye.

Chorten, Muktinath

A castle of souls,
a song of sublime stones
in the timeless manuscript
of racing winds and rain shadows,
cotton puffs of clouds drunk
from rugged symmetry of brown rocks and Dhaulagiri peaks.

You could pass by it,
gasping in the thin air,
a fledgling flame,
an angry oracle mourning over
the loss of fruit and fiber,
roots and blood-red geraniums' ripe reminiscences...

Or could stay a moment,
place a pagoda of your breath on its crusty rim
or an oval black stone
to the shrine of shining stars
to consummate an ample union
of moon and sun in broad daylight.

A crumbling jar,
a terracotta horoscope
of hope and history,
you could earn a quiet morsel
of compassion as God's blessed food
to be dropped into
your father's gaping mouth
that remained open
even after he passed away,
right after his return from
a decade long ramblings along Naga ascetics
in the forests of rain and rites

What feeds the furnace?

driving the demons on a damp day away,
a conical kettle bubbling on an ancient stove,

ready to whistle away any moment
as you unmake your bed, fold sheets,

the wooden floor crackling underfoot
your kind host sleeping away into late lethargic mornings

not just a Park Slope pavement
a fire truck cracking the silence of a million eons,

screaming its way through
a quiet Sunday silence of 7th Avenue,

a half-burnt toddler
crawling through the hallway,

a sole maple leaf
serrated, magenta, autumnal

on the white strips
of a rain-washed zebra crossing

a deadly ambush in the scuffling eye
with the hound of my boyhood

even on a dusty Himalayan street
as you walk teary-eyed and

someone you love hands you
a prize soaked in an acid of insults

what guides your shaking hands across
the scrawny page of your late mother's wrinkled face

banishing the ghosts of gloom away?

Saligram, along the Gandaki River

In the canyon
of Brahma's daughter

before battle
between blue blur and black night

before Vishnu disguised
to trick a pious woman's nose ring

and got cursed
as a stone black,

black as his own guilt
black as her kohl eyes

fierce
and blind from insult

a touch of sesame seeds
and dried out blades of grass

a golden fish
aflutter in its fluorescent eye,

a lava of vermilion,
a constant reminder –

flesh is only a flame
soul hard as a humbled rock.

Eyes of Andreas' Chorten

Very human, hungry,
feeble, almost,
.
water like, fish like,
a just born baby's tear like

a charcoal geometry
on the palpable face of an upright glacier

pure and crystalline,
Christ like, before Paul's murky shadow fell,

bemused eyes
older than horoscope of Siddhartha,

larger than the ocean
a female Yeti would have shed

before she was grabbed
and butchered by the monks

defeated by
the daggers of compassion

yantras of Sunya,
throttled by Boddhisattvas

brutally wounded,
weary eyes of a human

buried beneath
debris of spiritual flagstones

and snow sheets
of savage civilizations

a ruthless tear
in a body, a bullet full of blood,

a rough hewn
creature grabbed first

thing in the morning
like Ganesha's head

and crucified before
it could have said a word

about history, mystery,
hunger and humanity.

I might be the last one

I might be the last one
to walk these trails littered with dry leaves

song of the rain falling
like slow sonorous river

the cicadas breaking
silence of green glades

the wind picking up its chorus
skittering through the barley fields

boulders strewn
along the trail by the noisy river

shrill chir chir
of the lonely birds

and the dung fly
buzzing around the head

a sad reminder
of the cities I've left behind

sapphire ponds
a mirror for Phurba's eyes

the villagers bringing
glistening water buffaloes up the crooked mule paths

mossy boulders
velvety gossamer green beneath the maple trees

and a twig
laced with flowers of my youth's lusts

laid across the path
like a prayer wheel

an invitation
to the elusive tip

of the snow mountain
leading to the kingdom of eternal snow.

Beef

I chew the meat chunks
from a floral soup bowl and ask myself—
Doesn't it seem strange but familiar,
a tinge of a taste I've had before?
She's making stuffed tomatoes,
my kind hostess in her plush Brighton Beach apartment.
I slowly chew the softened fiber of the slices
and slurp at a spoonful
of soup along with crusted bread pieces.
My first hour in the city,
just came in from JFK.
Before taking a yellow cab,
ordered a cup of tea in the waiting lounge café
as I always do and asked the gay couple
sitting next to connect me with her and here I am.
She came in from her office right when
our cab arrived; we took the elevator
and I put my coat and bags away.
The air on the way was crisp,
with a flare of blue patches of the ocean on my way.
But what meat could it be, I ask myself.
"I will soon go out," I tell her, "thank you for this treat,
and do some grocery shopping."
I remember today is Deepawali, the festival of lights.
I left home early in the morning
on a very auspicious day, " You never leave
when the goddess is supposed to visit your home,"
my brother had said. But I have landed
in a different time zone now, I console myself,
gods are different here, even demons,
many have ruddy orange faces and wear red neckties.
Then she brings a plate of stuffed tomatoes
and I ask -- What meat is this?

"Beef of course" she blurts in her Russian accent.
"I am a Jew, I don't eat pork."
My jaws drop, I try to forget what I have just heard.
I try to reconcile, try to make up for the loss,
"It's okay when you do not know about it,"
my mother would have said. "O Kake, how would
you have known ." in her deeply wounded voice.
And on top of it, it's a different time zone, I believe,
I am on the other side of the earth,
the Himalayas down below, actually right under my feet.
Do our Gods hold any sway here? I ask
and sleep reluctantly on the bed
she has made in the guest room
and recurrently dream of oxen chasing me
across the river of blood. Next morning,
I wake up and spread my hands,
The first thing I always see in the morning.
I see a rash seems to have appeared on my left arm,
and during the day I notice it spread like a calamity.
Is it bed bugs? Is it pollen?
I ache in pain, as the cherry grains appear all over,
my belly, my palms and knuckles, my butt and
then I remember the goddess that my mother said
was angry and had entered my body
when I had a similar rash in my childhood,
probably measles. She is raging,
so keep quiet son, pray, do not touch it,
or think of it, she will pass through your body
like an angry wind or a wave of a troubled ocean
and perhaps never ever return.

The Alchemy of Nine Smiles

One

From now on, Mom,
every moment would
become a miracle.
Your mourning face
trapped in a circle
of daggers would turn
into a nine-petalled dandelion.

Two

After Nag Panchami,
after the last of the Monsoon showers,
after feeding the serpents
of the cursed valley of fiery dragons
from the earthen bowls
full of milk, saffron and honey,
they would start winding
sacred threads round hysteric torsos.

Three

The sleeping shamans
of the fuming valley would
wake up from their torpor
of rain and rhymes and go stomping
the squelching streets, furling
their skirts along with feathered crowns,
beating their drums to kick up
the drooling pulse of my numb body ...

Four

They would wake Shiva
as he sleeps after a catastrophe
of lights of million galaxies triggered
by his favorite consort's uncouth hands
asleep now with her endless menstrual flow
in a separate smaller pond,
whetting blue waters of a turquoise lake
in the high Himalayan canyons...

Five

The copper bowl
the priest dropped last year
in the lake up above
would be found here again.
Crossing a million hill ranges,
it would arrive today
to dot the blank spot
on the city's fluttering calendar.

Six

Your face would appear again,
Mom, a nine-petaled dandelion
or the flame of nine burning suns
smoldering in the dusty streets
of the Republic in the making.
You would appear
again on a decorated cow,
your voice louder, shriller.
You would smell my head,
tousle my hair, hold my shaking frame,
aching endlessly from the erratic
wheezing of demented dolls...

Seven

Nine months ago
when you left me,
for months I slept on the spot
they gave you your last shower.
Nine months ago,
agitated and angry,
you moved about in the hushed spaces
of our ancestral house.
Every morning you sat on the threshold,
chatting up the women who passed by
tirelessly unstitching the quilts of the house,
opening up pillows, cushions, blankets
and tearing down the fancy dresses
especially tailored for your numberless gods and goddesses,
quietly sobbing the absence of your son,
and of your man who vanished years ago
on the trail of hashish smoke
along the blue rivers flowing
into the shrieking forests of despair...

Eight

Tomorrow again, I know,
I would see you riding
a bejeweled cow I donated in your name,
almost a decade ago.
I would see you agitated
in the alchemy of your fresh avatar;
your voice thundering,
your eyebrows knitting
mandalas of forgotten mantras
of my fretful moves
in numbered streets of the famed cities...

Nine

Nine different dresses
I would put on tomorrow,
eat nine colored foods,
visit nine shrines,
drink from nine rivers,
nine water wells,
feed nine holy cows,
nine crows, nine dogs,
and utter your name nine times
along with my children to shake
the poise of Shiva sleeping
beneath nine boulders
of nine glaciers, making
his nine consorts bring
nine smiles nine times
on your face
in memory of
nine precious months
you kept me in your belly
and patted me
nine times every month
in the flowering of nine-petalled
dandelion of your youth.

Where would my story end?

For Amanda Bhabhi

In the crevices
of a cracked paradise

jolting from
an elastic energy

trapped in
the earth's sanguine womb?

A heaven tilted
sideways, the paralytic

face of a hillside
grandma left out in the cold

by dim-eyed demons
of a flailing polity?

They predict a disaster here,
a future fractured

from the accumulation
of an ocean of a molten mass,

a divine frenzy,
a reversed vision

of the earth's own unmaking ,
retracting herself into an island again

a Jambudeep,
an island of eternal Vedic hymns.

Someday, they say,
the earth will change her side in sleep,

exasperated from
a turbulence in the reservoirs

of kinetic energy,
shaken from a vision of an impending doom,

an Ajeema / a Harati
our primordial mother goddess

of numerous off-springs
burying her own squealing new-born

beneath the weight
of her hefty torso in the whirling

black tunnels of her post natal sleep...

Geophysicists, panelists,
prophets of the whimsical West

pundits of the twisted East.
I see them squinting into the fogged holes,

imagining a cosmic crash
in the valley of the Lord himself...

But where's there a way
for me to desert it, and end my grand story,

my Himalayas, my continent,
like my own destiny,

a life suspended in mid-sentence
a journey in smudged lanes of century's crooked sleep,

the broad-chested canyons,
the glaciers melting like tantrik trophies

from the Master of Time,
Padmasambhava's snow sanctuaries

full of the thawed bodies
of bleary-eyed wanderers reeking of hallucinating yantras,

hubris of consuming
fresher fragments of newer galaxies...

What if tomorrow,
what if this very moment

Kailash opens up,
tearing up the carpets of white rabbits

racing along
the green pastures of the shining lakes,

what if Lord's own
pinnacle of patience crumbles

and newly found republic
turns into a tiny morsel

in the jaws of a mighty
dragon of an apocalypse?

Where, I wonder,
then would my story end?

Nirala Series

New Books

Kailash: Jewel of the Snows
Rajinder Arora
ISBN: 978-8193936719 Paperback 2021 pp 268
plus 68 color Demy

A Short History of Nepal
From Ancient to Modern Times
Shreeram Prasad Upadhyaya
ISBN 9-788182-500174 2021 PP 255

Mother's Hand: Selected Poems
A Bilingual English/Nepali Anthology
by **Jidi Majia**
Translated into Nepali by **Yuyutsu RD Sharma**
ISBN: 978-8182500174 Paperback pp 96 Demy

Dancing in Place: *New Poems*
S. Renay Sanders
ISBN ISBN 81-8250-048-6 2019 pp. 64 Paper Demy

Blue Fan Whirring: *Poems*
Mike Jurkovic
ISBN 978-8182500969 2019 pp. 160 Paper

Imagined Secrets: *New Poems*
Robert Scotto
ISBN 978-81825000442019 pp. 79 Paper Demy